These Four Walls

Selected Poems

Bernadette Wolff

Full Court Press
Englewood Cliffs, New Jersey

First Edition

Copyright © 2003 by Bernadette Wolff

Published in the United States of America
by Full Court Press, 601 Palisade Avenue,
Englewood Cliffs, NJ 07632.

ISBN 0-9709477-9-8

Line drawings on pages 136 amd 140 by Bernadette Wolff
Author photograph by Umberto Esposito
Cover and book design by Barry Sheinkopf
Colophon design by Liz Sedlack
Cover photograph, "Door, Key West," Copyright © 1995 Barry Sheinkopf

ALSO BY BERNADETTE WOLFF
Live Bait: A Novel

FOR MY DARLING GIANNA,
whom I love with all that I am,
was, and will be.

"It's my party, and I'll cry if I want to. . ."
—Leslie Gore

Table of Contents

Short Skirts
and Varicose Veins

"So-and-so's Mom's flipping out,"
my daughter tells me.
"She's wearing short skirts
and chasing after younger men—

hanging out in nightclubs, smoking pot,
and when she's too zonked out to drive,
she calls her daughter to come get her."

I raise my brows, heave a sigh,
picture a woman
with jowls, frown lines,
and jiggly thighs
in a miniskirt
on the dance floor,
shaking her arthritic "groove thing".

"Thank God you never did that,"
my daughter groans, eyes down.
"It's *so* embarrassing."

I smile;
finally
we agree on something.

In a Bar

In a bar, a man of sixty
sits plastered,
cursing his dry season.
Like a hawk,
he hovers over a set of lasses
who snub him.

Across the way
another woman sits,
chunky and rouged, matronly—
willing to sell her charms.

He eyes her through
the grey smoke
blowing hither and yon
and, as he raises an eyebrow,
tips his glass.

Her laughter's
like a horse's whinny,
and she nods.

He struts up,
plops down next to her,
says hello,

too drunk to know
they once had sex
in the back seat of a '57 Chevy.

Crooked Eyeliner

I was nervous
getting ready for work,
knowing she'd be there
hovering over my every task,
sighing, criticizing,
catching my errors,
and while applying my make-up,
I smudged the liner.

Imagine,
with work to be done,
looking out of skewed eyes
all day long.

Black Book

"She's the one," he said,
falling in love with her instantly.
"Now I can throw away
my little black book."

And she took him
for better or worse,
but later found that,
when women wear,
when their bones grow brittle
and their hair goes limp,
men's fingers wander
back through their yellow-paged memories,
forever young.

First Day on the Job

A man who's learned
to be his own physician says,
"I'm doing peritoneal dialysis at home."

"I placed three liters of dialysate
in my belly the other day,
and I'm exchanging only
one-point-five.

"My speed diffusion's off.
What do you think?"

I glance at his feet,
swollen as a slug
on a rainy day,
skin livid, cracked, oozing.

What do I think?
I ask myself,
and my problems fade.
I shake my head and whisper,
"I don't *know* for sure.
I'm *new* at this."

Under My Skin

The whole world's gotten under my skin—
you, the dentist, my hectic schedule
even the food I eat
is poison nourishment,
giving on the one hand
and taking away with the other.

How can the world ever get right
when my own cells are attacking one another,
little men-at-arms
on a search-and-destroy mission?

For three long years I've swelled and flushed
and, once or twice, lost consciousness.
"Idiopathic," the doctors have said,
"chronic urticaria."
Meaning: Hives, of origin unknown.

I came to only to realize
that it may never be over—
the lumps and bumps,
the itching, the scratching,
the fire kindling beneath my skin,
the wondering. . .
what if, next time, I don't wake up?

These Four Walls

When you knocked on my broken-down door,
asked how I was, I answered with a smile.
Pathological liar that I am,
I said, "I'm fine."
The words left my mouth like ticker tape.

"I'm taking stock of that which doesn't kill us.
In other words, having a pity party.
No frills, just me, dead silence,
and these four walls. . .
Join me?"

You left, of course, weary of reclusion
and still in need of stroking—
and I went back to weaving half-truths
like, "I'll be fine."

"Chin up," I said to your back.
"Time and patience will crack that nut."

I Don't Sleep Nights

Beneath the dusty granite skin
and tangled wire veins of our Fallen Giant,
there's a staple gun, a piece of desk,
a photo of someone's child,
and no one to claim it.

On this side of the river
come the orphans,
infant refugees who need mothers,
and I run to be the first on line
to offer my breast, my blood, my comfort,
as if these could erase
the hell that's rained down on us.

And while I do this,
I dare not gaze
at the gloating cloud of smoke
that clutches at our skyline,
or acknowledge those
who rush to snap their photos
of this cement-and-body masterpiece
that I never want to see again
because I don't sleep nights.

Englewood Girls

I envy a woman
whose every hair's
in place,
with makeup fresh
into the twilight—
one who doesn't sweat
at the gym.

I pound away
at the treadmill,
suck back my Evian,
bodily fluids oozing out
over my upper lip,

observing some rich man's
prized possession—
her dainty, coddled form,
her tittering voice,
bipolar eyes,
no street fears I can see—

and wonder
what it might be like
to come from there.

Stolen Glance

I caught you
from the corner of my eye,
checking the twitch in her hips
from the corner of yours.

I thought you said
you didn't like
painted women.

When I Was Forty

"When I was forty,
I looked twenty,"
you said to me
through jaded lips,
as if to remind me
that you were once
young and beautiful,
as if to warn me that,
though I was marrying your son,
I never could replace you.

Your Claim
Has Been Denied

In my mind's eye,
I could see
her pinched nose,
her tight, smirked lips,
as she declared triumphantly,
"Your claim has been denied."

"Anything else
ya wanna axe me?"

I replied,
tight-lipped, too,
"Yes, I *would*
like to axe you. . ."

Facing Changes

There was a time when I took
long black hair and firm thighs for granted.
I'd laugh at Mom
for falling asleep in her chair,
not knowing where she'd left her keys,
for dishing out advice.

I went on with my life
somewhere between those years and these,
and yet, now, clinging still to my yesterday me,
I pant on the treadmill,
reminding myself between breaths
to rush to the beauty salon,
squeeze in a touch-up,
and, wondering whether I left the gas jet on,
suddenly realize that
I look and act so much like Mom.

Artistically Inclined

"She's artistically inclined,"
the matron was obliged to say,
but really meant "eccentric",
"*outre*",
"nuts", perhaps.
"She can dream up the most extravagant stories.
It's a gift, you know."

And solemnly,
the psychiatrist smiled,
knowing that mothers are like that—
always looking to find
the best in their children.

Good Luck Charm

Whenever something good happens
while I'm carrying or wearing
something different,
I take it everywhere;
consider it a good luck charm,
like the time I met my husband
at the gym, which is why
I slipped you
that smelly old spandex thong
when I first saw you
dancing with the redhead.

Closing the Door

"Don't let the door hit you in the ass
on your way out," you said as I left,
as if I had no right to walk away
on all you'd said and done,
as if I wouldn't be better off alone,
leaving you with no one but the cat
to boss around,
who never listened to you either.

Good Timing

Good sex is like good comedy—
timing's everything,
and when you caught me
at the stove this morning
by surprise, my back turned to you,
and you groped my breasts,
(my youth gone,
and the mystery along with it)
your timing was perfect.

Refugee Poem

I thank God
when a poem
breaks loose,
gets out
on its own—
not so much
for the sake
of catharsis,
but for the poem itself,
for God's allowing it
to escape
from the me inside.

For Allan, My Therapist

You crack my shell
like a walnut,
and I wait inside
to be eaten,
then thrown up.

Humpty Dumpty

Humpty Dumpty
had it good.
After his fall,
they did
what they could—

tried to piece him
back together.
But after I cracked,
you changed
like the weather.

Cold Egg

It had been years
since I had given any thought
to making love.
I acted icy, distant,
utterly obsessed with getting by—

but all it took
was one short look from you
to heat me up.

I left
in a sweat
before you could notice,

like a cold egg
just out of the fridge
on a summer day.

You've Got Balls

"You've got balls,"
I nearly said
when you rang my bell
seconds after
I'd slammed the door
in your face
for being with her.
"You've got *balls*."

Woman Scorned

I read in the news
a woman scorned
had let loose hundreds of roaches
in her ex's apartment,
and later set the place on fire
with him in it.

And to think, all I could do
was cry the day you left.

Getting Pudgy

"You're getting *pudgy*," he said.
"Better watch what you eat.
You should exercise more.
Don't want to get fat, do you?
I wouldn't like that."

"I suppose I *have*
been hitting the sweets too hard,"
I sighed, and gulped.
"Must be something missing
in my life."

Convincing Myself

I've been standing
before the mirror
for hours,
getting ready for you,
wondering why it's taken
months for you to call.

The doorbell rings;
I notice a grease stain
on the hem of my skirt—
the good one.

Knowing you—
the perfectionist,
a stickler for punctuality,
I suck the edge of my hankie
and rub it over the spot,
convincing myself it won't show.

Nothing to Wear

"I haven't a thing to wear,"
said the Jewish princess,
reason enough
to decline his dinner offer.

"I can't remember
the last time
I went shopping,"
she sighed,

poor thing,
her closet door
half-open,
stuffed with items
from upscale boutiques,
tags still hanging on them.

Classic Black

You knocked at my door,
asking to borrow
my black sheath—
the one with tucked seams
that I wore to your wedding.

Thank God,
they never go out of style.
I had it kept
in the back of the closet,
hoping to someday
fit into it again.

Until you tried it on
and zipped it up,
I'd forgotten
how nice I looked in it.

A Poem

A poem's elusive,
there or not—
flies in
like a butterfly.

How could you
have just told me
to sit down
and write one?

Like a new life
waiting to be born,
it knows its time.

And can I
now give birth?
Can I hasten spring?

Twin Gifts

(for Eugenia and Barry)

Twin gifts, you are to me—
as cherished as a set
of golden bookends
reaching to embrace
a classic tale.

Like a book, you know me.
When my spine crumbled,
you held me erect,
smoothed out my pages,
coaxing me to make it
through the final chapter.

Who Am I?

Decades later,
we met out of the blue,
but you forgot my name.

Somewhere between the groping,
hedging, hemming and hawing,
I suffered a death of sorts.

Suddenly, all that I was and am
shrank into a nameless face
in a void of time forgotten.

How foolish:
All along, I thought
it would happen in reverse—
that my flesh would fade,
and only then the memory of me.

New Chapter

(for Harry and Ellen)

"Think of it
as a new chapter in life,"
my friends said.

But a chapter in a book
should follow a sequence,
not strip you of your whereabouts;
and the event of your death,
my darling,
has hurled us into opposite worlds.

New chapter indeed—
a new book altogether,
perhaps, and one I wish
I'd never been forced to read.

Oh, No

"Oh, no," you said,
"you're not writing
depressing poetry again,
are you?"

"No one wants to read that crap.
People want to be entertained.
Can't you, just *once*,
write happy poetry?"

"I suppose so," I sighed,
"If I could just
get this goddamned knife
out of my back."

Easy for You

You don't know
how tough the road
can be to hoe.
Walk a mile in *my* shoes
then come tell me—
you with your perfect,
smooth, pedicured feet.

Just a Habit

"Why do you do that?" I ask.
"Why do you put me down?
Why, every time I try
to build self esteem,
do you point out my faults?"
And you say, "It's just a habit."

Unsure

Because I wasn't sure
when I received the invitation
whether I'd be going
to a wedding
or a funeral,
my RSVP read NO.

The Scream

(for Daddy)

In the pitch of night I woke,
and like a howling wolf,
I screamed your name
as if you'd hear me
from the grave.

You let me know you had,
and it was decades overdue.

I'm My Mother

Never thought I'd see the day
when my lips would finally say,
"I remember days of old
when children weren't quite so bold.
When I was young, I listened good–
the way a nice young lady should."

Offering thus, this hackneyed quip,
Self-consciously I bit my lip,
for when my daughter grinned her grin,
I saw the trap I'd fallen in.
"I'm my mom!" I cried in grief
and a touch of disbelief.

Had I, in fact, behaved that way?
Never thought I'd see the day.

Jackal

I should have seen it
in your eyes,
but my guard was down,
and when I put my heart
in your hands,
you ripped into it
with the teeth of a jackal,
grinning,
proud that there was
one less beating
in this world.

Hendoko Yaku

"Change poison into medicine,"
a Buddhist told me once.
Nearby, he pointed to a wounded bird.
Couldn't get off the ground;
it just kept spinning
in a circle,
flapping dirty wings,
giving me hope.

The Dress I Wore

Cleaning out the closet,
I came across the dress
I wore the night
that you proposed.

The faded smell
of your cologne still lingered,
but your face
I could barely imagine.

Special Edition Barbie

"I know you're feeling bad
about your mom going so fast,"
I was saying from across the room,
when I suddenly realized
his attention was elsewhere.

He had on a soft porn channel,
appeared to be drugged by some blonde,
hair down to her rear,
perky, firm balloons,
stretch marks protesting
the silicone assault on Mother Nature,
scars pulling,
groaning against her areolas.

She was slim-waisted,
with painted lips,
fingers, toes—
and, God knows, *uninhibited*. . .

And I remained invisible,
hair as limp and dark as pitch,
every bit the night
that she was day.

Eyes downcast,
I whispered,
"At least she didn't suffer."

Nightmare

Even after I awoke
with a start last night,
that dream wasn't
going anywhere—

hung around me
all day long,
like a stale odor,
like the nails
of a rotted corpse.

Five Pounds to Go

Only five pounds to go,
and I'll be
the same size
I was in high school,
when we met
at the senior prom
and time stood still.

I still have
your class ring;
it fits tight
around my finger—
so tight, time
couldn't loosen it.

Broken Record

Like a broken record,
you repeat, "Me, me, me,"
having worn the "you" out
while you were busy
dancing with her.

Like All the Rest

"You're just like
all the rest," he said,
disgust in his eyes,
to get me to buckle under.

It almost worked.
For a second,
I wanted to erase his
painful other women—
be for him
what they were not—
until I remembered
he'd once said
I was his one and only.

A Run in Her Stocking

She looked confident
on the unemployment line,
not at all like someone
who had just been fired:

Bloomingdale's suit,
Macy's hair and nails,
Saks shoes,
and a run in her stocking.

Chanticleer

Each morn I hear the chanticleer,
a most impressive sermoneer.
He stops to say I sleep too late.
He's right; I tend to vacillate.

I lie and think, Should I awake?
And then I start to bellyache,
"Oh, Chanticleer, go back to bed,
you ornery old featherhead.

"You are an uninvited guest
who knows I need my beauty rest."
After all, it's Saturday,
and I'm not due at work today.

So off with you,
you noisy cock,
go bother someone down the block.

I Don't Have To

"I don't have to do anything
but pay taxes and die,"
I said, eventually.
The seven months of therapy
had finally paid off.

"You're *fired!*"
my boss declared.
I gathered my things
and left.

Guess I showed *him*
a thing or two.
Now I don't even
have to pay taxes.

Beautiful Day

"Look at what
a beautiful day,"
I say, eyes closed,
lying back on a hammock.

"Sun's shining,
birds are calling,
and each blade of grass
is velvet green."

"Are you nuts?"
you ask me.
"It's raining like *hell*
out today."

"Ah, yes," I say,
"but not on the inside
of my eyelids."

I Lingered

I lingered in bed this morning,
things running through my mind,
trying to will away the past,
the present, and my future fear,
and then I rose,
went about my day—
head still nailed to the pillow.

The Cat

These days, the cat
is my constant companion.
Wherever I go, he follows.

I read the newspaper,
and he drapes himself across
the mound of my shoulder.
As I crochet, he rests
in the crook of my arm.

When I do laundry,
like an *enfant terrible*,
he sneaks into the dryer,
and every time
I open the closet door,
he runs in there to play.

With adoring eyes,
he follows me everywhere,
much the same as the children did,
many heavens ago,
before they outgrew me.

Learning Disabled

(for Rob)

"Pervasive developmental
disorder of childhood
with autistic features,"
they said gently
when you were three,
careful not to rock my boat.

"He's learning disabled."
The doctors grimly nodded.
"Probably never understand
well enough to be on his own."

I reeled from the softened blow,
unsure whether to mourn
your doomed emancipation
or celebrate eternal innocence.

Almost There

It's no fun
to be starting out,
no joy to be finished,
over and done—
but to be "just about",
to be close,
to be virtually,
within a stone's throw
of anything life has to offer
is what I live for—
the elation,
the anticipation,
the suspense of being . . .
almost there.

The Eleventh Hour

Thunder booms:
a purple sky
with jagged streaks
that drive the wind
wailing through trees.

Rain drills the earth to mud,
and animals scatter for shelter
as each blade of grass
floats belly up—
revenge for an early spring.

Thin Ice

The minute I set foot
on that pond, I knew
I was skating on thin ice,
but the thrilling fear of it
flung my blades across that glass horizon
and, for those few moments,
I was as weightless as the wind!

Looking Glass

My looking glass has finally said,
"I like exactly what I see."
Between us, you and me,
the wrinkles are there,
the gray hair's coming in,
forty's just around the bend,
but I don't care—
I like me now.

When I was young,
my life was cocktails, coifs,
executives and poets,
restaurateurs.

I had fancy dresses,
ribbons in my tresses,
la vrai couture,
parties galore.
What used to be *haute cuisine*
has suddenly turned lean.

But I know me now;
I didn't then,
and I can say
my looking glass

is finally proclaiming
me in what I see.

Many Long Years

Many long years ago
I said I'd always love you
although you never believed it.

I've yet to forget
those hazel eyes,
that hair so china-black,
the lips like pillows,
kissing another's mouth.

Words Unsaid

His final breath
was a sigh
of unsaid words,
his last rusty tear
spoke for itself,
knowing he'd never told her
how he loved her;
and fate didn't give a damn—
just let him die
as randomly as he had lived.

The Widow

"How long did it take,"
I asked a widow of ten years,
"for you to get over him?"

"I'm still not sure I am,"
she sighed,
and I knew then
love never dies—
it takes the core of you along.

The Way of the Wind

Some follow the sun,
others the moon;
but I've gone
the way of the wind.

I've left behind
the tried and true
in favor of uncertainty,

sidling through leaves,
whistling among the trees,
tinkling wind chimes—

an Autumn vagrant
settled only
on the here and now.

Inside Out

Now and then,
I think of you.
Why must this be?
They told me everything would pass
and soon I'd be back to normal.

But I'm no fun at parties anymore.
I only laugh on the outside.
Should someone mention you
I brush it off,
but to think what might have been
still hurts inside.

I hope, at least,
you're happy now—
both out and in.

Forget-Me-Not

It was the amethyst flower
of fragile form
that caught his eye,
having blossomed
from a perfect seed.

She turned to face him
as he nearer drew,
and, smitten so,
he plucked her from her bed
before she could be trampled
by a roving foot.

Each spring thereafter
has left him wistful
for the Forget-Me-Not.

Elegant in Death

He was elegant in death
as not many of us are,
accepting his fate
like a gentleman.

He spoke of his wish
for my future success,
bade me good-bye,
and left with a smile
as I groped for some composure
with which to inter him.

A Jealous Streak

"Watch that man,"
Mom said, to my surprise,
after he'd left.
"He has a jealous streak."

I could've sworn
he'd charmed the pants off her
with his flirty tongue
and sparkling wit,

but all along,
it had been *she*
who charmed *him*
with a glass of warm milk,
homemade pie,

got him talking,
then caught him,
pants down—
unaware.

Relationships

STAGE ONE:

He's smitten, she's oblivious.
He woos, she hesitates.
He keeps up, she succumbs.

STAGE TWO:

He's clever, she's impressed.
He promises, she's doubtful.
He delivers, she demurs.

STAGE THREE:

He's competitive, she's apprehensive.
He thinks, she feels.
He's smart, she's dumb.

STAGE FOUR:

They argue, make up, and marry.
She wins, he loses.

Anniversary

I set back the clock
when idle time weighs heavily,
when winter seems to linger—
and, in the beat of a heart,
I'm young again
with a summer glow,
and there you are
with eyes that promise a future.

The Waiting

For more than a lifetime
I waited for you,
time sifting through my fingers
faster than sand from an hourglass;

my youth stole away
but my heart kept vigil,
bloomed when we met—

an alien rose
in acres of barren land,
where it thrives still
on our love.

Tunnels

(for Don)

It was the light in your eyes
that saw me through my tunnel,
taught my anxious heart
a new regard of love.

And now that death attempts
to boast its triumph,
let it be the light in my eyes
to see you through.

Darkest Hour

(for Don)

Through the darkest hour
I lie awake, wondering
if you'll be there
when morning breaks,
watching your body wind down
like a clock losing time.

Your every ragged breath
sinks my heart deeper,
and though I beg
each passing moment stay,
I know that time
is not on our side.

Hear me now,
as our breaths still mingle:
if you should go
and I should stay,
I'll die each day
until you dry my tears in heaven.

Hourglass

Our love's an hourglass,
each falling grain of sand a vow
that tumbles from your lips
into my soul.

The Kiss

His pillowy lips find hers,
and raven hair,
thousands of heavy strands,
fan from their roots
when his soaring fingers
race from crown to waist-length end.
Her weighted heart
lifts with them.

Untwined

At the foot of our bed
you pluck my hairpin,
unraveling licorice strands
that curve at my neck
and blanket my breasts,
covering what you love best,
but loosening my inhibitions.

Phantom

He doesn't know
that when he left me
at the door this morning,
blowing a kiss as he waved,
my body went with him.

Never Enough

In the dusk she comes:
long red fingernails graze his back,
seasoning her fingertips
with his zest.

A lasting sting remains
where she licks
shivers up and down his spine and,
between her gobbling kisses,
hears him cry for more.

Flagrante

We turn in bed and yawn,
our neighboring thighs
gathering yet again
after a long night.

Canaries warble
in the morning light;
admiring them,
the kittens purr.

Yes, we're in love.
They're talking about us
without us knowing it.

Fire in His Kiss

There's snow on the roof,
yes, hard to miss—
but I'm warm and cozy,
sighingly prosey,
kindled by the fire in his kiss.

The Edge of the Bed

When night comes,
you sit at the edge of the bed
and, like a faithful pet,
wait for me.

I undress, rambling on about my day,
the things that kept us apart—
laundry, shopping, telemarketers.

"I'm not me anymore," I gripe
as I crawl in beside you
and switch off the light,
"I'm a list of things to do."

Drawing the blanket up under my chin,
you peck my cheek
to soften the bite of darkness.

May/December

Damn the years
between us—
so many demons
bent on meanness.

As angels hearken
in heavenly chorus,
let's count the years
that lie before us.

A Thought

"I don't know what's worse,
your nightmares
or your poetry,"
my husband mumbled
when I woke him
from a deep sleep,
middle of the night,
to tell him
a thought
had finally come.

Housecleaning

I took our wedding album out today,
blew off the dust, leafed through
the pages of our years.

Time just seemed to fly.
Never made it to the vacuuming,
the laundry, so many other things
that life, I'm sure, intended.

Dense Fog

"There's a dense fog
out there," you said,
having returned
from your early morning jog.
"Careful driving."

I nodded, poured the coffee,
and you read the paper,
leaving me to wonder
how long it might take
for it to lift.

Lip Service

"I'm sorry," you said,
ears flushed,
day after
having called me
a "stupid bitch"
during an argument.

"I love you," you said,
tapped a foot,
awaiting a response.

"I said, 'I *love* you',"
you repeated and,
dwarfed by the sick, naked
perversity of love,
I cleared my throat,
whispered, "You, too,"
and nodded,
the sting of it all
still in my veins.

I Haven't Been Able

I've been wanting to write
but gangly words
rise up like a newborn colt,
fidgety ideas form,
but my pen pauses.

If I knew what was going on inside,
I could choke it out,
but I've had to keep
a distance from myself, and—
cloistered numb
in this pending state—
haven't been able.

Rainy Days

I awoke to rainwater
leaking all over
our expensive new white carpet,

spoiling what it took us
years to achieve—
all the sweat and blood,
the dirt and grime
that we endured,

the struggling
to recreate this innocence—
all wiped away
by one quite random act.

We Talked
like Strangers

We talked like strangers
after that unkind word,
not knowing where to go from there,
what else to say—
yet understanding
one unkind remark begets another,
we kept our silence.

Now, I suppose,
if poetry begot poetry,
I might end this spat,
but what you've said
burns still in me—
I have no clever words to offer.

My Biggest Fear

My biggest fear
is not a life alone,
or eating out of cold soup cans,
or calling no place home.

My biggest fear
is not about the scars of yesterday
or of the things tomorrow may yet bring.

My biggest fear
is that you'll
never understand
what you have done to me.

Hard Lessons

What did we teach our son?
That love is a figment, a celluloid myth.
That marriage is a war zone.
That familiarity breeds contempt,
passion dwindles, hatred lingers.
That respect wears away, in time,
like a rock in a brook.
Already, I'm lost to my grandchildren.
He'll never marry, you know.

Faded Ink

Going through old papers,
I came across our marriage license
and noticed the ink had faded.

Does it matter?
It isn't worth
the paper it's printed on—
I never read between the lines.

Twiddling My Thumbs

You left me
to twiddle my thumbs
while you went off,
deciding whether our marriage
was worth saving;
before that,
I had never even known
that I was all thumbs
when it came to you.

Bed of Nails

This life of mine's
a bed of nails—
each mocking word of yours
sinks into me
a fraction more,
although I know
that, if you left,
my heart would stop.

You Were Cold

Your eyes were as cold
as a body on a slab
when you said
you were leaving.

I shuddered to think
how far we'd come.

Cold Coffee

Been inside out all day—
almost lost my breakfast
this morning, when,
out of the blue,
you snapped
about your coffee being cold.

I held it in
but when you left,
I spilled my guts
in front of the mirror
about other such
cold coffee breakfasts
and how they came to be.

I like mine hot, too,
and my toast crisp,
and my bacon lean—
but you've never noticed.

The Occasional Mouse

Problems arise in our marriage
like the occasional mouse
I spot zipping
across our basement floor.

And like that mouse,
I dodge the broom chase,
hoping to find
a hole to climb into,
a safety zone,
where no one can
kill my young—

No one like you,
their father,
who left us long ago
in that cold, dark basement.

Generic Love

Time has passed
since we vowed our love
in voices like thunder
from the skies above.

How could love
that once was stable
begin to read
like a comic fable?

How could love
that was enigmatic
ebb and wane,
become so static?

Was it real
from the start
or a fleeting, common
affair of the heart?

Empty Threat

You tell me
that, if I leave,
you'll die—
an empty threat
to keep me as your pawn,
a ploy, an act
from a wax-skinned mannekin
long past dead
in my eyes.

All for Show

You kissed my cheek
on your return
from work today,
but it was all for show.

You winked
as the kids looked on,
you nodded,
asked, "So what's for dinner, honey?"
all the while
fondling secret thoughts of her.

When Are You Gonna Learn?

When are you gonna learn
that it wasn't about *you*,
it was about *us*,

and that
it was never what *I* did wrong,
it was what *we* did wrong,

and that, when they said,
"For better or worse,"
they actually *meant* it?

Why can't you see
that it'll all be the same
with your new "she"?

She'll become me,
and you'll still be you.
Unless you open your eyes,

you'll just repeat your life,
and love will pass you by
as you go on

blaming me for your past
and her for your future.

Waste of Time

I remember it began the night
you said everything would be alright.
Since then, it hasn't been the same;
we took to one, long, silly game.

Looking back as I write this rhyme
I see it was a waste of time.
You cannot hear, or just don't listen
when I complain the crystal doesn't glisten.

And when I try to clean the dust
from our wedding photo, as one must,
you hardly ever pay attention,
hardly ever even mention.

"Was it all a waste of time?"
I ask, no longer in my prime.
"What lies ahead for you and me
with children grown so handsomely?"

Now that they've gone, I see
the silence lasts for an eternity.
Shall I say good-bye and simply quit
a love thus rendered counterfeit?
Or shall I stay for habit's sake?

I'm tired of making this mistake.
I've passed my prime, but I'm taking time
to buy a crystal vase or two
and shine them till they look brand new.

Not Strong Enough

And to think
I told those lawyers
everything—
all my secrets—
deadens me.

Yet deep within these veins
I know
that what they warned me
now is true—
you'd dance on my grave.

Old Skin

Tonight,
I shed my gold band
like old skin and,
with it,
decades of sorrow—
remembering how you,
years back,
slithered between my sheets,
coiled round my heart,
squeezed out my last breath,
then tossed me off for good.

All That Glitters

"All that glitters is not gold,"
Mother warned
as I approached my womanhood.
I scoffed, told her to mind her business,
found a lover with gentler words,
pretty flowers, trinkets.

By the time he slipped a diamond
on my finger, I thought,
this must be love.

Yet now, as we head for divorce,
I gird my loins and turn to face Mother,
who's been watching, all along,
from the bleachers.

Fencing Hangers

They struggle in the closet,
the fencing hangers,
like gnashing swords.
I gasp as I look on,
reminded of how we used to be.

Absolution

Alone, naturally,
I stood before the court,
confessed our differences,
telling how we'd stayed together
for the sake of children,
grown now,
who'd never appreciated the sacrifice.

The black-robed judge sat high up,
unemotional,
and paused before the gavel cracked,
echoing in the tall-ceilinged forum.
"I absolve you from your marriage,"
she said,
as if our years together had been mortal sin.

The suited strangers never flinched
when the tears struck my eyes
or when I glanced at your empty seat
for a last good-bye.

Alone
I shed my grief before them,
my relief,
tears for everything divided,

the yesterdays of bad choices
and paid dues,
tears of hope
for a bright tomorrow—
God and the judge willing.

Alimony

Is it a token of honor
for years of unrequited love—
a purple heart?

Or, like the menses,
more a monthly clue to barrenness?
Could it be a booby prize
for being taken in by your suave lies?

Why must I feel like a beggar?
Should I envy the widow
whose grief seems more noble than mine?

If I don't sign this check,
will I, only then,
be worthy of your love?

Making Friends
with the Devil

"Keep your friends close
and your enemies closer,"
Mother warned me, but I,
young and oblivious,
went on my merry way,
meeting up with devils.

Finally,
I married one,
thinking,
how much closer could I keep him,
totally misconstruing
what Mother had meant.

Carnival Plane Rides

Earthbound—
I let her fly today,
and there she is,
soaring on the air—
checking over her shoulder
to make sure I'm still watching.

I don't fly,
but who am I
to pin her down?
I see the rose's thorns;
she, nothing but the petals.

Mothers and daughters
differ so:
Her eyes are wide,
the wind whips though her hair.
It looks like fun.
I wish *I* could.

Nickels and Dimes

These days, you seek me
out of need, not love,
asking only for money.
Remember when you'd run to me
with bleeding knees and pouting lips?
I had a pocketful of kisses to heal them.

But now, when I ask,
"What's grown between us?"
You roll your eyes, you tap a foot,
too old for kisses.

Still, I give freely of all that I have,
glad, in some small way, to be needed,
knowing that, one day, you'll drain me dry,
and I will have no legacy to leave
but these few words from a beggar
who spent her life
trying to buy your love.

Speaking Our Minds

"I *hate* you," you tell me,
and I, dumbfounded,
ask you why.

You say I'm a know-it-all,
a meddler, constantly nitpicking.
And for this, my darling,
you rip yourself from my womb?
What's a mother for?

Someone Else's Child

(for Rachel)

I've been to hell and back
where you're concerned,
yet it still hit me out of the blue
when you said,
"She's like a mother to me."

I swallowed those words
like razor blades,
thinking,
but I *am* your mother!

Then I remembered a young girl
who once described me the same way
to her own mother, and I saw
how much easier it is
to know someone else's child.

Booze, Cigarettes, and Trojan-enz

I don't want to be nineteen again,
when those idols studded my shelves
like a mark of bounty—
puffed up on some ruthless,
headstrong quest for individuality and love
that got me nowhere.

I'm wiser now
in ways I never thought my mother was,
and I've put those days aside,
lived them down.

But now,
my daughter forces me into the past,
and I see me in her eyes, her ways,
and, neck hairs bristling,
shudder at the sight of old scars
from self-inflicted wounds.

Under My Roof

(for Rachel)

Years ago, Mother said,
"As long as you're under my roof,
you'll do as I say."
I left, of course.

And now, I wring my hands,
and, struggling through tears,
I try so hard to not say
just those words to you,
but they slip out
in angry haste,

and off you go,
leaving me
to make some sense
of our newfound freedom.

False Hope

When you lived inside me
my heart danced on the hope
that our paths and souls
would ever mingle.

I kept faith in my dreams
until that savage day
when you chose
to be without me.

All I have now is a photograph
of an infant at my breast,
in whose eyes I glimpse
my own reflection and,
realizing how natural it is
for a mother to forgive and forget,
I weep.

Everybody's Different

"How long did it take
for the ache to fade
when you kicked out your son
for good?" I asked,
feeling some guilt
about saving myself
from a destructive parent/child relationship.

"That was it," you answered,
your hand moving in a flat line.
"I did it and never looked back."

Two years and still hurting,
I sighed, "Everybody's different."

Thanksgiving Day Blues

Such stillness
as the sun withdraws,
leaving shadows
on old turkey bones
cooked for a guest
who never arrived,

and the silent phone
that shrieks of memories
from days gone by,

when the sweet rush
of your tiny feet
would preface the whisper
of those precious three words
that, today,
you didn't care enough
to call and say.

Belated Mother's Day

I could tell
when you arrived
three days late
with a Hallmark card
that you hadn't given much thought
to selecting it.

No flowery words,
a hasty signature—
it'd been chosen
from the rubble
of other mothers' loving children,
orphaned, so to speak,
at a clearance sale,
as if your love for me
was half-off.

Predestination

Why, of all things,
when I was desperate not to,
for practical and logistical reasons,
did we have that family portrait taken
two days before we parted?

It was as if fate
offered a haunting record
of happier times.

The Closer We Get

Together, we've traveled
the harsh roads you chose,
and I held you up, cheered you on,
cushioned your falls,
pushed myself to live your life,
until, one day
it got to be too much.

When I collapsed,
God whispered in my ear
he was trying to teach you a lesson
and that, if I didn't get out of his way,
he'd put me down.

In my silence, I realized
he'd been shouting this for decades
and I hadn't been listening,
but older, wiser, and calmer now,
I can see that the closer we get to our graves,
the more readily we commune with the Divine.

A Mother, a Daughter, and a Granddaughter-to-be

(to Rachel, on Christmas Morn, 2000)

I awoke feeling different today.
My scars have faded, my tears have dried.
As I look around me, the darkness is gone.

The dissension between us has melted away
like a snowflake against the wind.

The infant girl within your womb,
has unlocked the riddle
that we fought so long to solve:
that love finds a way,
and that, swiftly, life goes by.

In the heralding of her arrival,
we're forced to rid our nests
of our cliches
and see us both as women.

You, a blooming rose
abandoning your schoolgirl dreams,
and, I, older, yes,
but not too old to bend,
join hands for her sake.

Children

Children are a noose
around your neck
that one day bring you
sweet breaths
of fresh air
called grandchildren.

Tickled Pink

(for Gianna, on March 14, 2001)

They hand you to me,
bundled soft and damp,
your cheeks flushed pink,
fists tightly grasping air.

"It's a girl!"
Tufts of black hair
moistened still from birth,
your wandering eyes
coast mine,

and the blood dances
in my veins,
my heart bloats
as I cradle new life
with my bare hands,
feeling *happy*.
I mean really, *really* happy.

A Sleeping Child

(for Gianna)

If ever there was a heaven,
it's in the slope of your lips,
in your tender grasp,
in the stillness of your smile
as you lie,
fast asleep,
in the curve of my arm.

A Summer Tan

(for Gianna)

Like a summer tan,
you feel warm and cozy—
your newborn flesh
a tonic for my wrinkled cheek.

And when you leave,
when the door
closes behind you,
I ache for more—
dreading those winter months
when you grow older
and away from me.

Growing Old

(for Gianna)

All my life, I'd been rushing,
rushing, rushing,
too busy to notice
that time spent like this
had made me weary.

Suddenly saddled with aching feet
brittle bones, jaundiced eyes,
I saw only my losses
and wrinkles in the mirror.

But just as I thought
my best days were done
you came along,
the glow of trust in your eyes
an elixir
that redeemed my sense of wonder,
restored my youth.
How could time have known
I needed a grandchild?

Don't Touch That

"Don't touch that,"
I'd tell my kids.
"If it breaks,
Mommy will have
to pay for it."

Good mother that I was,
I kept their fingers scarce
in china shops, in toy stores,
near somebody's pet.

I was lauded by clerks
and parents alike
for my child-rearing skills.

Decades later,
there's a grandchild and,
"Why do you *spoil* her?"
I'm asked.
"When I was small,
you never let me touch a *thing*."

The toddler's eyes
volley between us;
I speak first.

"Go ahead,"
I say, "Take it.
Grandma will pay for it."

The Maple Tree

(for Daddy)

Lay me under the maple tree
where the grass,
like an armchair,
safe and worn,
is veiled in shadow.

I've spent hours there,
drenched in dew.
My eyes close,
and your face appears;
your voice lives
in the rustling leaves,
consoling me long after
I awaken from the daze I'm in.

Such a Tease

Dad was such a tease.
It was his way
of showing his love.

Still, I cried when he said
my face would freeze
if I didn't stop scowling,
and I smiled when he called me beautiful
despite my frizzy braids,
thick lips, heavy glasses.

And on the night he lay dying,
when he said he'd be gone by morning,
of course, I thought
he was only teasing.

Girl Lost

I cry whenever
I recall the little girl
who had Dad's devil eye,
Mom's pretty smile.

They say that death
is part of life
but these days,
I can barely tell the difference.

Chances are
I'll see her in my dreams tonight,
awaken, dry my tears,
and think of her again—
the girl that I once was.

Some Things Hurt

(for Paul)

Some things hurt
more deeply than others.
I've learned that
by comparison—
like when we were young siblings
and you slapped me hard
for playing with your army men,
and then
when we grew
and you left for Nam,
returning more harsh and cruel
than the enemy himself,
leaving my heart
a deeper shade of purple.

Written at Grandmom's Gravesite

(for Marietta DeCostanza)

As she goes to dust,
I see a fraction of her glow
rise through the ground.

I'd seek to rouse her,
break death's sleep,
but know the earth
needs her.

With a phantom hand,
she strokes away my grief
as I fondle scraps
of her history—
a cherished, stoneless ring,
a lock of her hair . . .
it makes a woman weep.

Remnants of Grandpop

I was expecting your death
but it came as a shock
when I went back to your place
and your things—

the clock that stopped
at the hour of your passing,

the old fedora
with your sweat stains
ingrained on the rim,

your motionless wooden cane,
a pack of Camel's, unfiltered,
that turned your fingers brown—

they mocked me now, so I thought,
as if you'd used them up
for O so very long
and they could haunt me now,
take on the life
you left behind.

Lucky Woman

Lucky woman
you are
to have that man.

He worships
the ground you walk on
and,
aside from his interest in me,
he'd have no other.

Lucky woman
indeed,
Mother.

The Thought
of Her

The thought of her
cracks my heart
like an eggshell.

I tried to warn her,
but she danced on
in her dusty shoes,
losing focus.

How she loved life,
that glimmering girl,
though hers was littered
with unwon battles.

She died struggling
to show her face to the sun,
and I,
no more a woman
than I was when in her womb,
closed my eyes to cut it off,
just as I always do
when reading sad poetry.

Think about Yourself

My mother,
inveterate philanthropist,
gave me sage advice one day,
said, "Think about yourself.
No one wants you
when you're down and out."

I was shocked to hear it.
It had taken her 78 years
to realize this,
and I wonder how long
it'll take me to listen.

Awakening

(for Mom)

For so damned long I spent my life
making everyone else's comfortable . . .
just like you.

It was you who taught me
the godly things—
to be giving and caring,
to turn the other cheek.

Now, you say
your son has opened your eyes,
made you see the light,
see people for what they are.

Shoved away in a nursing home
for too damned long,
now, Mother,
you tell me to think about myself.

Big Five-O

I knew I was riding
on the slippery slope
the day Mother
forgot my birthday.

I'd made it
to the big five-o—
no cakewalk, aging—
and she wasn't there
to share it.

Her fading mind
had dramatized
the years collecting
on my birthday cake.

Fifty lit candles
couldn't brighten my day.
I let them melt.

Everyone held their breath
as I ran to the phone
and called Mom
just to say
it was a beautiful day—

the sun was shining,
the grass was green,
and I loved her.

Like a Lamb

Like a lamb to the slaughter,
Mom went into that nursing home,
resigned to obey
"God's will"—
as if he had created
that hell for her torture,

as if it were he,
not we,
who signed the papers.

Tucked Away

"Tucked away," said Mom,
when she went, prematurely,
to a nursing home.

"When you can no longer
do favors for people,
they just tuck you away."

Being a good Christian,
she took it on the chin.
"'Vengeance is mine,'
sayeth the Lord." She nodded.
"And just you wait and see—
sometimes, if you live long enough,
you get to watch him dish it out."

Getting On

When I last saw Mom
in the nursing home,
her fists all balled up,
supported by a metal-armed wheelchair,
head hanging low, her twisted form
tethered there to prevent
yet another fall, I thought,
Genes are contagious.

"She's getting on,"
I mentioned to the janitor,
excusing her condition.
"Happens to the best of us."

I was taken by surprise, though,
when the bubbly nurse appeared;
"You must be Rachel's daughter!"
she remarked.
"My God, you look just like her."

We Make Our Beds

"We make our beds,"
Mother would say
when I was young,
"and then we lie in them."
It rang with wisdom and clarity,
although I had no living
to relate it to.

She taught me well
about cooking, cleaning,
making beds.

I followed in her footsteps,
falling into the good-old-fashioned-girl trap;
and by the time I thought,
not once, but twice
about our fireside chats,
she was in a nursing home,
talking out of her head,
her face as white as a sheet,
lying in the crumpled,
hellish prison
of the bed she'd made.

Time to Go

Plastered smile,
I suck in a breath,
ask, "How's my girl?
Ready to go?"
Mom nods, silent,
on the trip home.
A week's vacation
at my place isn't enough.

Arriving back
at the nursing home,
she looks away, unforgiving.
I hurry her past
the hallway biddies,
their heavy-lidded eyes
and clucking tongues,

flirting with tomcatting grandpas
in wheelchairs,
who purse their spittled lips,

and I curse my impotence,
knowing this is the best
I can offer—this, for Mom,
is Home Sweet Home.

I Smell Old Age

I smell old age,
Mother,
infirmity,
in this nursing home.
It's just not you.

I remember
your sweet scent—
the fresh milk
that I nursed from your breast,
the powder-puff talcum baths,
the anisette in your demitasse,
so *Italian*.

These odors aren't you,
Mother;
you don't belong here.
Let's go.
It's not what Daddy
would have wanted.

My Mother's Ready

We've had our talk;
I know she's ready,
yet still I pray
to keep her here,

tenaciously opposed
to stepping up
next in line.

I Kneel in Prayer

Mom always said
I was too selfish,
too headstrong
to acknowledge her wishes,

but I have come to see
how right she was about everything
from brushing my teeth
to choosing men.

And now that her past
has slipped away,
her future's dwindling,
and only pain is here to stay—
more constant, more abiding
than any daughter could be—

I kneel in prayer,
at her request,
for the favor of her death.

From Early On

From early on
it was your voice
that echoed
through the water,
soothing me.

And when the water broke,
I reached the open air
with chilly flesh,
unfocused eyes, ears radar sharp
for the sound that charmed me.

Now, when I am
on the verge
of being me, singing
at the top of my lungs,
you lie mute
in the hands of an undertaker
who has taken great pains
to stitch the lips that told me stories,
sang lullabyes,
lips that will soon
be buried alive.

Alphabetical Index of Titles